THE
LOVE
LIST

Sonia Poleon

The Love List

Choose Your Partner

Sonia Poléon

Published by Sonia Poléon 2016

For more visit www.TheLoveListBook.com or join the email list at www.TheLoveListBook.com

ENDORSEMENTS

"Grab your copy. This book gives you a whole new perspective on the 'dating game', teaching you to positively use the tools you already possess, enabling you to reach your end goal of becoming Mrs Right to your very own Mr Right. For a short read it's packed with advice, techniques, it also has exercises for you to complete to assist you with compiling your very own Love List. A brilliant read.

You go Girl, told you already I love it."

Sandra Barnes – *Criminologist*

"I wish I read this book before I had my many red flags, thanks Sonia for setting out some critical thinking about what who I am , what I need and what I want need and desire. I realise that my needs are different from my wants . Having read this book, I have gathered enough information to now make an informed decision about who I want to spend the rest of my life with."

Ava Eagle Brown- *Multi Award Winning Book Stylist, Coach, Speaker & Actress.*

www.avaeaglebrown.com

TABLE OF CONTENTS

The Love List, Sonia Poléon

"Create the biggest vision of your life and put your partner in it!"

- Sonia Poléon

DEDICATION

To all Single Ladies who have in the past had relationships that didn't work out for whatever reason: Be comforted by knowing that all those relationships were meant to be, that they were part of your learning curve, that they happened in order to teach you so embrace them. Learn from them knowing they were a part of your destiny. They have been instrumental in shaping the amazing person you are today. Those life lesson relationships have made you into the best version of yourself in preparation for the man who was made to love you, and he is just round the corner. Hold firmly.

If you hadn't had those relationships, you may not have known that you needed to create a Love List.

ACKNOWLEDGMENTS

MY FAMILY

To my beautiful daughter Chevali Poléon and her three children: Thanks for being proud of me. You keep on going and I will meet you at the top. I will be there to pull you up.

To Savannah Poléon: Bright eyes and bushy tail, you are so talented and clever, that's my beautiful granddaughter. I know will be very impressed and overjoyed at what your nanny has achieved. Love you, Sav. xxx

To Nioka: I send messages every week reminding you of my radio show. You threatened to block my number. I once said, 'When I am famous, you won't want to block me. 'You responded saying, 'You are famous, and yes I will still block you. 'Thank you for your whiplash. www.ACalmBirth.com

To Adam: My eldest son, I remember the days when you used to eagerly and excitedly be waiting for another article to be published in the local newspapers. It took longer than expected, and when it came, it wasn't quite in the form you anticipated. When it did come, your kind words were 'Well done.' Thank you, my son. x

To Cavell: My baby, you always encourage me. When I am feeling down, you get that YouTube out and start sending me inspirational videos to watch. Thank you for encouraging me and for believing in me.

MY FRIENDS

To Gillian Paul: Many evenings I stayed over at your house while you studied and I wrote my book. It seemed like a good idea, but then you would sit at the table chatting and distracting me. Even though I didn't complain and I also took part in the communication, my mind would fervently think about completing this book. I thank you for all your love.

To Patrick Reid: What can I say! You have always believed in me. Even when I doubted myself, you never doubted me. We have been through lots together, and you have always been there. Thank you for caring and sharing. You are one of my besties, oh yes, and my 'Mentor.' www.PatReid.co.uk

To Darren H.D. Jones: Thanks for all your encouragement and for taking the time to send me a 10-step message outlining exactly how this should be done. At times we don't realise how much we impact the lives of those around us. Thank you for your advice and for believing in me.

The Love List, Sonia Poléon

To Janet Blair: We have had very similar stories in our lives, but through it all we continued to smile. Thank you for seeing the light that shines in me, even when I couldn't see it myself. Thanks for being a listening ear even when I kept you up late telling you all the things I am going to write about. You could have told me to shut up, but instead you turned your listening ears on and gave good encouragement. www.TheJanetBlair.com

To Sandy Campbell: You are a little gem, and I want to thank you publicly for the incredible patience you exercised with me. You have this innate ability to understand a person and give sound advice and guidance. Thank you for all the time you spent with me.

To Sharlette Reid and Anthony King: It was lunch time. I was taking my clothes to the dry cleaners. We stood at the end of the Mews and debated The Love List. Anthony, you believed that having a Love List would limit us that we shouldn't create one because our perfect match could be someone completely opposite to what we write down! Sharlette, you on the other hand totally disagreed with King, believing that it was most beneficial and important for a woman to have an idea of what it was she wanted. If not she could fall for just anyone!

To Matthew Lowe: Thank you for your input, you advised me to 'burn my Love List.' :-(

To Marjorie McFee: You worked for me for three weeks, which enabled me to attend my book writing course. If not for your help, I may not have been able to get this ready in time.

MY DESIGNER

To Dwayne Holness: For designing my book cover. I'm not the easiest of people to deal with, I know. Thank you for your patience and understanding. I know I am finicky and pedantic; I also know you are great at what you do and that you love a challenge. You always rise to it 100 percent. Thank you very much. www.IODM.co.uk

MY BUSINESS COACH

To Soji Fagade: My business coach, thanks for your valid input, for the endless hours we have spent on the phone or Skype over the past months and for the times you decided enough was enough and weaned me off of you. You understand me well, and for helping me creating this work of art, I thank you. www.SojiFagade.com

MY WORK COLLEAGUES

To Ingrid McLeod: Thank you very much for being a left-brainer. You never try to cut corners, and I appreciate your skills. You may get on my nerves at times, but I know you have my interest at heart. Thank you for holding things together at work when I couldn't be there.

To Clarevin Talbot: You are a little gem, and I appreciate your commitment and loyalty to me. You think I am amazing, but I too think you are amazing in all the work you do with the children.

To Nola Stewart: 'You left me just when I needed you the most.'(It's a song, but it is also true.) We spent a whole year together. You are wonderful, and I thank you for your encouragement and for the faith you placed in me. You are missed.

To Sherlon Thomas: Childcare expert, specialist and lifesaver, phew, thank God you know what to do and how to do it. Thank you very much for freeing up my time I was behind schedule, but you stepped up to help, which gave me back some time to complete this book. Thank you so much.

To Sylvia Grant: On all the days that I needed proper food to keep me going, you were there with your fantastic culinary skills, creating wonderful dishes, which enabled me to keep my strength up. Thank you very much.

To Fiona Nesbeth: What can I say about you? You are certainly a fireball, blazing everywhere you go. I would like to thank you and Keyshawn for your fast and furious ways.

To Shaniese Bryan: Thank you for the way in which you quietly come in and say your good mornings. You observe everything, yet you say nothing. You are a hidden gem.

To Laura Einecker: As creative as you are and as much as you love working with me, you seriously drive me crazy. But you know that it's all in the name of love. Thank you for your commitment to me and for all your help over the last year.

To my dear friend and buddy Steve Cabellero, who has been instrumental in helping me to understand what the requirements on my Love List means to a man. Many times I have sent over my changes and you helped me to define exactly what it would mean from a mans point of view, if it were not for you, I would never of thought about giving examples to each of my meanings, so thank you very much for your input.

The Love List, Sonia Poléon

To Agyeman Daapah: Again I would like to thank you for loyalty over the years, I just love the way in which you do your phonics with the preschool children, I have watched you grow and flourish over the years, keep up the good work. When you are gone home in the afternoon I often hear the children going through their phonics and teaching each other calling your name and making statements that you have taught them. Cheers big ears, and don't forget my shea butter!

To Karima Harding: You came back just when I needed you the most, yes it is a song but it is also the truth, I would like to thank you very much for coming back just in time. You coming back put the team back together again so that things could continue to run smoothly. Thank you.

To Pamela Greaves: My dear friend and "sister", you have been consistent over the years and we have shared some of our deepest and darkest secrets. On the flip side we have also shared some of our most exciting times together, done some amazing things together like get our first ever tattoo, I clearly remember locking the door so you couldn't get out ha ha ha! And of course we have comforted and been there for each other. Thank you very much for honouring me with your friendship over the years xxx

To my book mentor Raymond Aaron. If it were not for your book bootcamp I would probably not have committed to doing this book, we all have learning differences and my preferred learning style is in the classroom. Thank you for inviting this book bootcamp.

FOREWORD
by Claudine Reid MBE

It was Tina Turner's hit released in 1984 that encouraged women across the world to chime along to the powerful thought provoking theme tune " What's Love got to do with it?" The piercing words may motivate you to think about love on a deeper level. I mean what is love and more importantly what is the love list?

Your thoughts, fantasies, your deepest desires, your fears, concerns and perhaps wildest dreams can, in some cases be entwined in the theme of love, and the desire for a deeper relationship with your significant other. The person who understands you on every level, emotionally, physically, mentally, spiritually and sexually will be the person you want to share the rest of your life with. But before you find him you will need to know that these are some of the things you want in a relationship, that's why putting a love list together is important.

The love list will take you on a journey that will explore the key components for creating your list. You may feel you don't actually need a list. However given that you are in a position to want to live the best life you can, I encourage you to read with an open mind. If you are expecting a different result, then you have to do something different.

Over the past 15 years I have been working with women from a cross section of communities, we have talked about issues of the heart and the things that keep us awake at night, finance, children, love and relationships. The same questions keep on revealing themselves time and time again, what am I looking for in a partner, how will I know when he or he is the one, what am I bringing to the table?

Sonia Poleon takes an insightful look and makes some funda mental recommendations to women that are searching for their ideal mate.

The Love List, Sonia Poléon

INTRODUCTION

How The Love List Will Serve You

I think it's pretty safe to say that the majority of us women would love to get married. We want to enjoy the pleasure of being in a loving and trusting environment within a relationship, one that ultimately results in us having a fairy tale wedding.

However finding the right man is not like going shopping at your local supermarket, where everything they have for sale is on display and you have the opportunity to pick from what is available. No, there is so much more to selecting your lifelong partner than that.

Besides just imagine going to the supermarket and picking a husband, and you're stuck picking the best of a bad bunch! No, your life is far more important than that. You only have to realise its importance and put measures in place.

Of course this process for finding the right man will take a little longer than picking a husband up off the shelf. But this is the rest of your life we are talking about, not just the next couple of years. Surely the rest of your life is worth some effort.

Most women I know want to get married, even if they have been married previously - and if they have been married previously, then these ladies really know what they are looking for. But even if you have not been married before, it doesn't mean you are not in a position to choose the right person that is why you are reading this book.

Now we all know that there is no such thing as the perfect person; however in our heads, the perfect person does exist.

CHAPTER 1
WHAT IS THE LOVE LIST?

Our Shopping List

People are always intrigued when I tell them I have a List, especially men. One of the first things they tell me upon learning that I have a List is this: 'Choosing a relationship is not like going shopping.' Of course I know that, but when we go shopping, we have a list, even if it's just a mental list. A list, whether physical or mental, shows that we know what we are looking for.

If you were going to your friend's themed party, you would have an idea of what you wanted to wear. If you didn't, you would go out shopping to find something. Once again, when you're shopping, you're looking for something specific. You know what you are looking for.

Well shopping for a husband isn't the same but the theory is. We know what we want when we go to the supermarket, and it is just the same when we go out shopping for an outfit. Similarly when we are selecting a man, we know exactly what type of man we are looking for. Some women like certain features, like how a man is built. Others like other features, like bald heads, bums and so on. We have an idea of what we're looking for, though not necessary what his character is like.

Going on Holiday

And when you are going on holiday, don't you take the time to look through your wardrobe and all your summer clothes before deciding which items to take with you. You carefully pack everything you need in that suitcase, and you don't leave anything out. You even bring clothes for those 'just in case 'situations, even if you might not wear them.

How many times have you packed your suitcase, and then changed your mind about taking an outfit or a certain pair of shoes? You are choosy for a reason. You are making sure that when you arrive at your holiday destination you look good every single day. You want to look the best, and so even when you go shopping for your holiday clothes, you are very specific. You know what looks good on you, and you know what makes you look fat or ugly. Well you also know what type of man you are looking for, including what height, weight and the whole nine yards.

Don't you just love going on holiday the whole process - from choosing your destination to selecting the clothes to pack in your suitcase? There is definitely an air of excitement going on there, just like when you are thinking about the man you want to put on your Love List.

New relationships are always exciting - getting to know each other, the way he looks at you, the way you push your hair to one side, going out and always making sure you look fantastic to keep his attention and so that when he is with his friends they can tell him how hot you are. But before you get into that relationship you need to know what you want.

What's In Our Shopping Trolley?

Selecting items to pack in your shopping trolley and selecting items to pack for a holiday versus selecting the man of your dreams are very different selections, but no matter how you look at it, you are still going through a selection process.

[1] Amanda Chatel,Fox News Magazine, 8 Future Relationship Trends That Will Soon Become The Norm, www.magazine.foxnews.com/love/8-future-relationship-trends-will-soon-become-norm Accessed: June 2014

Most of us create a shopping list before we go to the supermarket, we write down exactly what we want so that we don't forget anything or put anything in our basket that we don't want. But how many times have we gotten to the cashier and realised that we have put more in our baskets than we anticipated. We forgot to put something on our list, we just simply couldn't resist something, or we change our mind about something we thought we wanted. Creating your Love List is again very similar to this process. As long as you have an idea of what you want then you can start the process and not be worried about what might change while you shop. Knowing what you don't want is half the problem solved. How many times have you had a certain item on your shopping list, but when you got to the shops you changed your mind? You are entitled to change your mind when it comes to selecting your life time partner as well. Come on! You are human; you have an active mind, and as time goes on, your needs change. So you can see how easy - and important - it is to create a Love List.

Eliminating Anxiety

Though writing a Love List might sound daunting, though you may be feeling fearful or some level of discomfort, the truth is it has to be done. Feeling uncomfortable or even anxious about creating your Love List is good. It indicates that you are moving out of your comfort zone and that you are really taking the task at hand seriously. This affects the rest of your life, and you have every good reason to be having mixed feelings. There is nothing wrong with these feelings, but you need to start.

But how on earth do you start writing a Love List?

Have you ever thought of a great idea but, not writing it down immediately, you couldn't remember the idea at all? In order to prevent this idea escaping, you buy a special notebook, keep it in your handbag, and when your inspiration hits, you can write it down.

You can do the same thing with your Love List. Anytime you think of something that should go on it, simply write it down. You can edit it later.

We have already discovered that we know exactly how to go through the selection process.

Preparing to Settle Down

Perhaps now you feel that you have been single for far too long, enough is enough, and you want to share the rest of your days with someone special. Though it might sound like a fairy tale, it's actually possible. Only you get to decide who that someone special is because only you have the power to choose in your life. No one will stop you because you will be unstoppable and unapologetic. You only have one life to live, and how you live it depends on the choices you make. Remember that only you - and no one else - are in control of your destiny.

You're feeling ready for a lifetime relationship, but ultimately before you can start sharing your life with someone else you need to really decide if this is what you want. Sharing your space with someone else is not an easy task. Where you used to hog the bed, now you will have to share it. If you are used to having the toilet seat down, now you will have to leave it up. If you are a workaholic like me, then you may no longer be able to stay at work until late in the night.

Often we have a wonderful idea of what we are looking for, but we forget to stop and think that 'Hey! maybe I need to change!' In order to attract the person you want, you yourself must start to be that same person. You need to know how to treat yourself well so that when you do find that special person he will also learn how to treat you well. If in the past you never really thought much about yourself, perhaps now you must start thinking highly of yourself. After all, you are the most important person in your world, and if you don't believe me, just go and take a look in the mirror.

To start treating yourself really well, spend some quality time with yourself. Go out on your own, and get to know yourself and what you really like. Date yourself, and learn about yourself just as you would a new partner or friend. By dating yourself, you will learn so much more about yourself, and who knows, you might even start liking you.

Is There Chemistry?

Physical attraction with your partner is definitely an added bonus in your relationship, and for some of us that chemistry is completely necessary in the relationship. However it's important to remember and understand that physical attraction alone will not be enough. After you two have gotten used to each other and you no longer see sex as an appeal, what will happen? Where does companionship come into the relationship? What kind of conversations will you have? Do you share the same goals, like the same things, go to the same places, and have the same friends? The list goes on. Physical attraction can only carry your relationship so far, and it is for this reason that you must be a seriously forward thinker. I know that when we women meet a man, we often automatically start thinking about the future: home, marriage, having a family, etc.but how much have we considered the person we want to share that life with us?

Remember we are looking for our soul mate, the person we can't stand to be without. I have friends who get anxious when their partners leave on business because they miss them. I find this very endearing, and I believe that's the way it should be! My friend Lola

Gordon often tells me she loves being right under her husband's armpits. That is so sweet. They have been married for over 25 years, and, of course, he doesn't mind. This partner you're looking for is one you want to have for the rest of your life. You may have already had relationships in the past that didn't work out, but now you are older and you are wiser and you are definitely more in charge of who you allow into your personal space. Ultimately chemistry alone is not enough to sustain your long-term relationship. You must remember to consider other qualities your future husband has.

Getting It Out of Your Head

You have an idea of what you want, but you don't actually know what the reality looks like. There's nothing wrong with that. You need a process to get from the idea in your head to the reality of a life-long, loving, and beautiful relationship.

Some people have never even heard of a Love List; they don't know what I am talking about. The importance of a Love List lies in taking pen to paper and putting some sort of shape to your many ideas. For example at the beginning of the year, many of us think about what we want to achieve, and usually we write down these goals and how we plan to get there. On the other hand, how often do we put pen to paper for our relationship goals?

Putting It On Paper

It seems very official and maybe scary or frightening to think that you have to put all these ideas you have down on paper. Just imagine if someone else sees this List! Oh my goodness, what will they think?

But I don't want you to worry about that. Writing your List down is a part of the process. How many times have you written out your goals, your plans, and your to-do list? We are just approaching this List in the same way. All you have to do is commit your thoughts to paper. It's as simple as that.

The more you ignore doing this step, the worse it will be. Once you have committed your Love List to paper, you free up space in your mind to think about other important things. Though committing this List to paper is not an easy task, it will be easier to evaluate, review and change things around to suit yourself when you have it all down on paper and open in front of you.

Even I have written down my own Love List, and every so often as I myself change and develop, I also develop my List. If I had let my List sit only in my mind, I would always be in a state of confusion and unable to remember what was important to me on the List. I have been able to change my List so many times throughout my life because I can see it clearly.

Some people have told me that I am confused, and some have said that I don't know what I want. Ultimately, however, these people are not me, and I cannot allow their comments to change how I feel about my Love List or what I want in a partner and out of life. They are not in my shoes; therefore they cannot even imagine how my life is or what I want out of it.

Remember that I said our needs and wants change as we change and that what we need and want all depends on what is happening in our life at this moment in time. So my advice is to take the time right now to commit your thoughts and requirements to paper and to physical write out your Love List. It might take you a couple of hours to get the outline written, but don't give up. This is your life we are dealing with, and anyone who comes into your life is worth waiting for and so it's worth getting this right.

Writing this List is like making a vision board, something we'll discuss in detail in the final chapter to help you take your List from goals to reality.

How to Start Making Your List

Of course, getting to write your List is the most exciting bit, really it is, or at least it is for me. Maybe you've guessed that I am an excitable person and that I just love new challenges and projects. Yes, writing a Love List is a project. It is another thing to put on your to-do list; but I want to make sure you complete it, do take time as there is no rush.

There are so many ways to actually start creating your List. I have tried a few different ways and have made my own formula and headings.

You don't have to follow mine. Simply think about what you want, and you can create your own formula and headings.

The Love List, Sonia Poléon

When I first composed my List, I only had two columns. They were (1) Must Have and (2) Can't Stand. I worked on that initial List for a number of months because it gave me a framework to start with. Just having two columns allows your creative juices to flow, it is easy to know what you want and what you don't want, and so if this helps you then feel free to use the same. However, as time went by, I realised that I hadn't actually incorporated any in-between qualities, so I added another section, called 3) Maybe. As I moved things around and put them under the various headings, I began to feel more confident about what I was doing and about what I wanted.

The more I wrote things on my List the more it developed and the more definitive it became. I changed the 'Must Have 'column to the 'Essential 'column. Here I put all the things I knew I could not do without. I had things in here like that he must be single. As a divorcee, I am actually free and ready to get married. I decided that I didn't want to be in a relationship with anyone that was only separated or who was in a so-called 'complicated relationship'. Either of these would indicate to me that he actually wasn't free and available to marry me. If I wanted to run off into the sun and get married, there would be a hindrance.

I started sending my List to a male friend, wanting a man's perspective on my Love List. He helped me to think about my List from a man's perspective. For example, I had written down that I wanted someone that went to the gym, thinking that it would be good to have a gym partner. However, my friend Steve noted that wanting someone who went to the gym could mean anything from a sporadic gym-goer with no commitment or self-esteem to someone egotistically in love with his own body and lives in the gym seven days a week. What was it that I really wanted? Umm, my mind started thinking, and I could see that it was best to change 'someone that goes to the gym' to 'someone who is health conscious'. The last thing I wanted was a man who thought the world of his body and didn't have any time for me.

The outside perspective helped me learn to think logically about what I want?, why I want it?, and the advantages and disadvantages that come with my wants.

It's Your List, Not Mine

Your Love List totally belongs to you and no one else. Only you have an idea of what you are looking for. Family and friends can give you suggestions, but ultimately you are the person that will be living with your partner for the rest of your life.

If this is the case, if it is we and only we that will be living with our partner, then why do we allow others to have such big roles in our life, especially when their lives aren't much better than our own?

Before you start taking advice from others around you, look at their lives, at their relationships, and see how well they get on with their partners. I personally will not take advice from anyone who has not been to and succeeded in where I want to go.

Earlier I mentioned that I consulted with my friend Steve. However, I consulted him not because I wanted him to help me to write my List but I wanted to know whether from a man's point of view if I was being unreasonable in my requirements.

Feel free to ask your friends for their valid opinion when writing your own List. Some of my best friends have not even seen my List, though I have been talking about this for a number of years.

The only people that have seen my List are those who I also helped in creating their List. Many of these women, I might add, are now married to their dream husband.

There is no one better suited to choose the right person for you than you yourself. After all, you will be the one committing to live with and spend your life with your partner. Don't allow others to influence your thinking.

CHAPTER 2

Mastering Your Own Romantic Destiny

Fairy tales teach young girls that before they meet their Prince Charming, they will first have to kiss a few frogs. But these stories never say how many frogs one will have to kiss before finally meeting the Prince. The good news is that you don't have to kiss frogs in order to find the man of your dreams. If you are 35 or older and still single, don't panic just yet. Use our thoughtful tips below to take control of your own destiny and find the man you will be madly in love with for the rest of your life.

Figuring Out the Kind of Man You Want

The first step to mastering your own romantic destiny is to figure out the specific kind of man that you want to settle down with, which is exactly why a Love List is important. Some qualities that you might want to consider might include similar cultures, values and goals; an ability to forgive as well as be forgiven and a desire to raise children, among other things.

Ask yourself where you want to be 25 years from today. What kind of person do you want to be in 25 years? How will what you choose today affect who you are then? Think to the future and be very honest. Follow your heart's desire. Know that the choice you make today will affect what you get in the future. Be very wise in your choices, and consider that what you find attractive today may cause you heartaches later in life.

Know Yourself First

You cannot successfully know what kind of man you want without first doing a self assessment of and really knowing yourself. Here are some tips for learning about yourself first.

• Make a list of the most important aspects of your own personality and life. The list may include things such as hobbies, ideals, goals and people. The most important part of this list is to be clear about the things that are important to you.

• Set goals for yourself. For example, if you want to get married in the next five years, make sure that the man you will be dating is also in the same place in his life. By knowing and setting your own goals, you ensure that your actions will match what you know you truly want.

Identify Key Traits That You Want Your Partner to Have

These traits can be professional, emotional and maybe even physical. However take care that you do not become obsessed with outward appearances. Ultimately, after knowing yourself, you must also know the kind of person you want in your life.

Consider personality traits that are important to you. For example, maybe you're looking for a person who is outgoing, optimistic, kind or funny.

Identify the beliefs you want to share with your life partner. For instance, it may be critical that the two of you have shared religious or political beliefs. Knowing this might even influence where you look for your potential husband.

Envision what you would want your partner to look like, but try to be open and realistic. While it is important that your man be physically attractive, do not waste much time searching for perfection. If you hunt for physical faults in potential partners, you will easily find them. Therefore focus on and be really confident about the personality side of your partner before considering his physical appearance.

Also consider occupational stability. You should determine what your future husband is like on the professional side. Do you want a risk-taking entrepreneur who globe-trots the whole world or would you be more at home with someone occupying a comfortable office job?

Take a Cue from Past Relationships

We will go into your past relationships in more detail in Chapter 3, but it is important to consider issues which you have faced in your past relationships that might have led to the relationships' downfalls. Issues that have stemmed from your previous partners are definitely things you want to avoid this time around.

Identify traits your ex-partner had that you found irritating or issues that caused the crumbling of your relationship. These may include simple habits or behaviours that negatively impacted your relationship. Refrain from dating men with such negative character traits.

Also know the undesirable qualities that you brought into the relationship yourself. Your ex-partner is not entirely to blame for breaking down your relationship. There are things that even you know you could have done differently in past relationships. Be honest with yourself, and think of the negative things that might have caused the relationship to falter. If you carry them into your new relationship, they could affect it again.

Napoleon Hill, author of Think and Grow Rich, is famous for saying that each of us is the master of our own destiny. We each direct, control and influence our environment. Whatever we want our lives to be, we can make it happen. This applies to more than just success or wealth; it also applies to marriage.

A happy marriage does not happen through sheer luck. It must be intentional. You must set your own goal, make a plan and strive to attain it. Not only does being intentional assist with internal harmony, it also enables us to get along much better with others. The best training ground to practice and develop these tools is marriage because your relationship with your husband will probably challenge you more than any other thing in your life.

Intentionality draws its roots from mind-body science. Currently, there is a lot of ongoing research to demonstrate empirically the power or potential of positive thinking. Become the master of your own destiny, and marry the man you want.

1. Set goals.

A great deal of psychology research[2] has proved that those who set goals are more successful compared than their peers who don't. Meanwhile many relationship studies indicate that shared goals play a very important role in the longevity of a couple. Setting goals for your ideal marriage demonstrates you have clearly determined the kind of man you want to marry. You will choose better, and you will never settle for anything less than the right man for you.

2. Resolve to prioritise your personal life

If you want excellence in your lifetime partner, you need to

---

[2] Fredrickson, BL. What good are positive emotions? Review of General Psychology. 1998

direct your romantic endeavours the way you do other things, like your workout routine, career or skin regimen. Through my own work as a relationship coach and a therapist, I have noticed that women who marry in their late 30s or later are the people for whom getting married carries the greatest weight. These women have often spent several years behaving as if marriage had no meaning for them. Later, however, it obviously does carry meaning, which is why it is important that you live and choose like you care.

3. Visualise your future in marriage

Everyone who succeeds does so because they first visualised their ability to prosper. By having a mental picture of yourself as a happily married woman, you come ever so closer to being a happily married woman. Do not regard your current singleness as a permanent condition. Instead treat yourself as a person who hasn't yet found her match. Believe that you will be married and that it's just a matter of time before you tie the knot.

While it is important to be grateful for the good life you live right now, it also helps to visualise how much richer you will be if you have a partner by your side. While you are very capable of accomplishing many things yourself, you can also let a man do

many of them for you and not feel diminished by his input. You are not pretending to be incompetent or weak; you are simply allowing other people to feel valued in a concrete and a direct way.

In the same way, you can visualise yourself make some changes so as to blend your life with your future husband's. Picture yourself moving to another city together or even being a stepmother to his children. The important underlying message with your visualisation is that you imagine yourself not always as a solo player but as part of a soon-to-be dynamic team.

4. Get rid of obstacles keeping you single

If you are older than 35 and still single, you either wanted to remain single until now or there are some things that have been discouraging people from approaching you. If you know what these obstacles are, then please go ahead and remove them. Pinpoint the hindrances that have kept you single and write them down.

It is possible that you just haven't met the right person yet. Another possibility could be that you have been busy acquiring an education or pursuing a career. Maybe you are able to admit to being a perfectionist, and as such nobody has come close to measuring up to your lofty standards. Maybe you ceased dating so as to prevent hurt and disappointment.

Whatever your reasons for singleness until now, be aware that answers that appear logical on the surface - such as perfectionism - could mask deeper issues you are carrying with you. For instance, it could be true that the right man hasn't surfaced, but maybe you haven't made many efforts to broaden your social circles.

Moving forward with your personal life is easier once you have sincerely assessed what's been holding you back.

5. Stand tall

Confessing that you would like to get married is not an affliction. It is just a defensible life goal. Put your pride aside, and let your friends and co-workers know that you are open to fix-ups and introductions to the right prospects. More often than not, we worry that sharing such desires will give us an unflattering or embarrassing light. Often wanting a husband is seen as a weakness or something shameful, but the yearning to bond with a like-minded partner is not a weakness but a strength. Meanwhile being introduced by a third party is probably among the best ways to land an appropriate mate.

6. Don't be too hasty in your judgment

Avoid jumping to hasty negative conclusions about the new men that you meet. It is easy to dismiss a man who means well if sparks fail to instantly fly between the two of you. The truth is that the really nice men - the kind, reliable, honest and marriageable material -probably will not blow you away on the first date. Go out with them a couple of times and give them a chance before dismissing them.

7. Disembark if the relationship is leading you nowhere

By the time you reach 35, you are dating not just for fun but for a reason. This simply means that you have to remove all non-marriageable men from your dating life. To stay on course, you need to ruthlessly cast off all narcissists, game players, mama's boys, professional bachelors and other lousy bets.

If you meet a man who is in his late 40s and has never married previously, you shouldn't expect that he will marry you.

The same applies to the man with whom you have been on and off for the last half a decade with no sign of commitment. Eliminate these nowhere men, and create room for genuinely marriageable guys who are just waiting to date you. The time you waste with non-marriageable men will never be recaptured, which is why it is important to do an early spring cleaning and remove from your life all energy vampires.

8. Live with gratitude

Fully appreciating the man that you have is probably the single most important way to get the most out of your life. You will feel more content if you wake up every day with an aura of appreciation. Being content even with yourself increases your positivity and makes you a magnet for others, even for marriageable men. If you aren't naturally appreciative and optimistic, you may want to practice being both.

Find small things that you can be grateful for everyday, even if you're facing singleness. There are many things that you probably take for granted that you should be feeling thankful for, such as a dazzling sunset or good health. Every day make it your duty to affirm the beauty of life and you will attract more of life's beauty.

9. Be patient

Searching for a husband is a slow and intricate process that requires a lot of patience. Though you may set a goal, it may not materialise in the exact same timeframe and manner that you plan. Be faithful and patient for your goals and dreams, and they will happen, especially if they resonate with you.

10. Take action

All of the above tips will amount to nothing if you cannot take action. It would indeed be very nice if we could just sit at home and let the universe fulfil our wishes and deliver them right to our doorstep. Sadly it doesn't work this way. You still have to take action. This will include doing all the above steps and also following up on opportunities or ideas that are presented to you.

Women Are Actually Ruling the Dating Scene

Though it might surprise you, it is women who actually rule the world of dating and relationships, as well as pretty much everything else in the world.

According to a recent study by EliteSingles, a whopping 71 percent of the women believe that they are the ones who decide how things will pan out in a relationship (Art of Manliness, 2014)

Whether there will be no date after the first one or a second date is left to the woman to decide. If she says no, there simply won't be another date.

In fact when it comes to ultimately choosing a husband, it is you who is the most important person to consider. Therefore learn how to take control of every date. *Remember you are single largely because you* have chosen to be. As women we have a wonderful ability to woo using our charms. In fact according to the same survey, 82 percent of the ladies interviewed were convinced that they can walk into a date and win over the man no matter who

---

[2]Fredrickson, BL. What good are positive emotions? Review of General Psychology. 1998
http://www.30everafter.com/2014/05/a-farewell-to-the-alpha-male/

[3]http://www.womans-world.co.uk/health-mainmenu-48/1378-women-less-lovesick-than-men-349823

he happens to be. If dates don't continue, it is because the woman decided so.

On the other hand, men do not possess such confidence in their ability to woo. Only 70 percent of men believe that they can impress a woman on the first date. Even more intriguing, only 46 percent of men believe that they have a say in the final outcome of the first date. (http://goodmenproject.com/featured-content/older-guys-lust-young-women).

Next time you are looking for a man, be the master of your own destiny. Below are more reasons why women rule the dating scene.

1. We have the upper hand

Science also backs this idea. In a dating scene, even if you have been pursued by a man, you are already 10 steps ahead of your male counterpart. Because a woman knows that the reason a man

---

[4]The Independent, What first-date nerves? Women revealed to be more confident on dating scene than men. http://www.independent.ie/style/sex-relationships/what-firstdate-nerves-women-revealed-to-be-more-confident-on-dating-scene-than-men-30224271.html. Accessed: May 2014

asked her out is because he desires her, the ball is automatically in the lady's court. http://www.blackdragonblog.com/2014

2. Men are kind of clueless

Dr. Wiebke Neberich, the study's director, explains that since men appear to overestimate the interest of a woman, they end up with more rejections than women do, leading to an insecurity that cannot be easily overcome. For men few things hurt more than being rejected by a woman. Rejection destroys them, and some may even stop asking altogether. Thus they often proceed to date with great caution, as well as a dwindling self-esteem.

3. Women know how to work it

Countless studies show that women are masters of seduction.

MASTERS OF SEDUCTION Beguiling Americans Into Slavery and Self-destruction Copyright © 2000 by Jeri Lynn Ball

http://www.devvy.com/

http://newmalestudies.com/

We know that what we wear, how we talk or even how we flip our hair can easily help us take charge of the matter at hand. It is just ingrained in our DNA. As women we are totally aware of what we need to do to make ourselves irresistible. In other words, we are the dating masters. So out there know full well that you can control the outcome of the date.

4. Women can be choosy

Women are a wanted creature! According to Dr. Neberich, women can be choosy when it comes to selecting a partner. There are many psychological and biological reasons to explain this. http://www.personalityresearch.org/

These reasons might explain the greater self-confidence that we identified earlier. Even in a city like New York, which has considerably more women than men, women can still afford to be choosy because we are the luscious fruits men want to pluck from the tree and devour.

5. Women know what we want quicker than men

Studies indicate that nearly 50 percent of women will know in the first 10 minutes of a date whether or not the man they are out with deserves further attention. Having this kind of quick insight is worth its weight in gold.

As a woman, I love the fact that my fellow ladies have so much confidence in their dating skills, not necessarily because of some kind of gender competition but rather because society heaps a lot of pressure on us. We have had to learn to adapt.

While the insecurity that men show on the dating scene is a cause for worry, it is something we can exploit to our advantage. Women are obviously more confident approaching a date than men, and this should give us the edge over them.

How to Get Him to Request a Second Date

We have already mentioned that whether you have a second date or not will entirely depend on you. That is to say that it doesn't matter whether he likes you on the first date or not. If you like him or if you would like to have another opportunity to get to know him further, you can make him ask you out on a second date. Below are 10 ways of ensuring that he begs you out on a second date, if, of course, you want him to.

1. Let Him Be a Man!

All the men that I know like to be the ones who make the first move. It is true that some men might be a little slow and others won't get the hint until you clearly make your point. Even if the man is slow, he is still the man, and he still wants to make the first move. If you know men well, you also know that they crave being in control. While it is okay to suggest the idea of a date, if you feel that letting him pick the date will make him happy, by all means go with it. Studies done recently have shown that the majority of failed relationships are initiated by men. http://goodmenproject.com/

2. Be Interested!

If you like the man you're seeing, you have to do all that you can to win him, and one of the things you must do is show genuine interest in him. While he's talking is not the time to start thinking about what your friend is doing or about what's going on in Corrie, even if he is not that great at talking. Do not hold onto your phone as if it's your first time seeing it. Give him all the attention he wants. Listen to him and respond warmly to show that you are following. You can even use information that he has told you or continue with a discussion he started. I can assure you that he will be very impressed. Make him feel important.

3. Be Friendly!

Another mistake women make is being too possessive. From glaring at any other females to wincing at every mention of another woman, it hurts to be possessive. Maybe you yourself have also dealt with a jealous boyfriend in the past, and so you know that it can be annoying. Please do not make someone else have to deal with a jealous partner, especially on your first date. Try to be as friendly and as open-minded as possible.

4. Let Him Pay!

Even if you have a fat wallet, it is the men who traditionally pay the bills. If he wants to pay, do not insist on footing the bills. If the man actually wanted you to foot half the bill, he would not suggest paying the bill at all. Just let him pay, and thank him for it. If you persistently insist on paying, it may indicate that you are trying to prove your financial independence; and if there is anything that men fear the most, it is the prospect of being with a financially independent woman.

5. Give Him Your Phone Number!

The majority of counsel on this matter will tell you to take his number and call him. However I advise that you give him your number and let him call you back. This way you are giving him an opportunity to call you if he's really interested and only if he's really interested. When he calls, you will have all his attention.

Meanwhile while you wait for his call, have fun with your friends and hobbies and continue living your life. Let him be the one leading the chase, and he'll be thrilled. This also saves you the anxiety of wondering when you should call him. Let it go, and let him make the call.

6. Arrange Dates!

Feel free to suggest activities or places for your dates. He may not always agree with your suggestions, but he will love the fact that you care.

Generally try to ensure that there are at least two days between the call and the actual date. This ensures that you don't appear too desperate, and it also gives him long enough time to miss you. It'll also give you ample time to pick a fancy sexy dress just for the date.

7. No Sex!

Sex on the first date is a no-no. Even if it has been too long since you last had sex, even if you are drunk or even if you feel very close to him, sex on the first date is prohibited. If you don't feel that you will be able to control yourself, do not even try to kiss him. Kisses and hugs are the closest you can go on that first date. If you were to have sex right away, he might get the wrong idea that you get too close to every other guy that you have a date with. Plus don't forget: men just love the thrill of the chase! Make him really sweat for it before you part your legs.

8. Treat Him Right!

Even if you and your date don't agree on something and end up debating on a subject you feel passionately about, make sure you always remain ladylike and respectful. Getting off to a fighting start is surely a dating blooper. Beyond just your date, make sure that you are respectful to everyone around you as well.

9. Be Honest!

While there are certain things you shouldn't tell him on the first date, make sure you don't lie about everything you say. Do not pretend to be somebody you are not. For example, you won't say that you love football simply because he does. If you lie on the first date and it ends up being a long-term relationship, he will find out, and won't that be messy!

10. Be Yourself!

Most importantly throughout this entire dating scene, remain true to yourself. If jeans are your thing, do not wear a suit just to impress him. If you cannot stand 90 minutes of football, don't meet him at a game. Put on your best and favourite clothes. From your trademark hairstyle to your own quirky jewellery, be as attractive and as personal as you can. This is the only way to make him fall in love with the real you.

You can download a free workbook at www.TheLoveListBook. com. Also, for more tips and information on finding the man of your dream, just check out the website above.

The great-grandfather of self-motivation Napoleon Hill says, 'You are the master of your own destiny. You can influence others. You can direct and control your own environment'. You have the power to decide what it is you want, which also means you have the power to make anything you want in life to happen, including a loving and meaningful relationship.

Napoleon Hill, Think and Grow Rich

You must decide what you want, make a plan of execution and put steps in place to make it happen. It sounds simple and seems difficult, but with focus and concentration, patience and faith, this should be pretty easy.

Be open-minded to the things that come your way because the things that you want won't always come to you in the form or manner that you expect.

Just as you drive your car to work on a daily basis, relying on yourself to get you there, so then you will manoeuvre your life too. Of course traffic will build up, but you know exactly what time to leave your home so that you don't get caught up in all that traffic. You can plan the same foresight in your life's journey.

Though we often think that it is easy to drive a car, we don't think about driving our lives. Many people simply drift down the river of life and go with the flow of the current, and when things don't go their way they wonder why! They have not made the conscious decision to be the driver of their own lives.

How many times have you changed your job in the past? Each time did you have to consciously make a decision to leave the old and move on to the new job? How many times have you moved homes? What did you do once you decided that you were going to purchase a new house or car? In any of these instances, you actively planned your destiny and exercised your faith in yourself and in that area of your life.

When we concentrate on the dominant thoughts in our mind, we are able to make our plans a reality. Whatever you believe is exactly what you will bring forth in your life, meaning that if you want a lifetime partner you need to have an open mind and stay focused.

Once you have decided that actually, yes, you do want to spend your life with someone, and then you only have to believe. Yes I said to believe. Even if you have been married before or have been in unsuccessful relationships, you can still find the right person for you.

You must desire to be in a loving and meaningful relationship. Many times people will advise others to relax and not think about it, and it will happen. However I am going to say the total opposite: think about it every passing moment that you have.

Just remember when you were buying those all expensive shoes, your lovely expensive time piece, or even that gorgeous car, you could probably not stop thinking about having any them until you actually had them in your possession. That is the power of your mind.

CHAPTER 3

The 5 Types Of Men Who Make GREAT Husbands

Marriage is very special, and the person you share it with should be also. Your future husband should be nothing less than amazing. When you find a man who exhibits most or all of the qualities listed here, you will know you have found a special person. Read on and take notes, ladies.

1. The Provider

Who he is:

This kind of a man always puts his family first. He is selfless and always strives to please the people he cares about most. This man can work two jobs and always find something to do in order to earn extra money, doing everything in his power to guard his hard-earned savings. He won't rest until he is sure that his family is safe and secure. He strives for excellence both at the office and also at home. This sort of man does not entertain words such as 'impossible', 'no' or 'I can't.' They simply don't exist in his vocabulary.

Why he makes a great husband:

With marriage, you start a new family: your family. Both you and your husband will strive to provide for this family. It is therefore critical that you partner with someone with whom you have similar goals. Having said that, there are times when a person may not be able to do what is required of him for the marriage or for the family, and that is the nature of life. Marrying a natural-born provider will be especially important when scales in the marriage tip.

2. The Rock

Who he is:

His strength not only keeps you stable but also inspires you during your most vulnerable times. While he is not immune to frustrations or pain, his handling of them is nearly heroic; and he knows how to get himself out of low times. This is the type of man that will never miss your call when he knows you need help or have something to get off your chest. He is a friend who will always be there when you need someone to talk to or a shoulder to lean on.

Why he makes a great husband:

This type of husband is devoted, loyal and a genuine pillar for the woman he loves. He is the perfect embodiment of an adoring husband on whom you can depend no matter the situation. What woman wouldn't want to marry her Rock?

3. The Critical Thinker

Who he is:

For this man, no problem - however big -is unsolvable. He is a quick and solid thinker, and he hates being pushed into a corner. He sees more than just the problem in front of him; he also sees a plethora of available solutions. When facing a new problem, he takes time to determine the best solution and how best to get to it. This type of man is patient because he realises that rushing a solution won't answer his problems any better or faster. He exercises great patience and is a mental champion.

Why he makes a great husband:

Despite the genuine beauty of marriage, it is not without its share of challenges and rough patches. Good times will not always lie in front of you, and getting back to the good stuff may require that you think differently. This type of husband makes a fantastic team player at times when you will only win if you are able to work together.

4. The Believer

Who he is:

This man would believe in sunshine even if it appeared as if the sun would never rise again. His faith is his foundation, and it is his faith that enables him to navigate through both the bad and the good in his life. This type of partner continually believes in the unseen things that other people give up on. He is God-fearing, and he is also very proud of his beliefs. He always has his moral compass turned in the positive direction.

Why he makes a great husband:

This type of a man has the essential emotional tools needed to fix many of cracks and crevices that are sure to arise in any marriage. He is a fighter who will not only fight for you but also for your marriage. He will not give up, not even when you do.

5. The Free Spirit

Who he is:

This is the sort of man with whom spending time never gets old. He believes that life is about living. He is therefore immune to the physical pains brought about by worry and stress, not because he does not feel these emotions but because he refuses to be consumed by them. He will always remain positive, seeking to savour all aspects of life. He chooses a career he loves, not necessarily the one that pays all his bills.

Therefore he is as passionate about his work as he is about fresh adventures. He likes traveling and most likely has a bucket list that is now at least a half-complete. This sort of man does not waste time fretting over what cannot happen. Instead he prefers to focus on what can happen. When you are with him, you won't have a dull moment. His inner light always shines through and warms the spirits of all those around him. This kind of man will keep life exciting at all times.

Why he makes a great husband:

It can be very boring to spend your entire life with the same person, always doing the same things. When you marry this sort of a man, you will literally eliminate one big challenge of marriage: boredom. Although it sounds like a simple problem, it is very important.

Why You Need to Think Carefully About Whom You Marry

Like her or hate her, you have to give it up to Sheryl Sandberg, who encouraged women to practice a lot of caution when it came to choosing a husband. According to Sandberg, the most important decision that you will ever make is whether you will get married and to whom.

Though she received a great deal of criticism for her comparison of marriage to a business relationship, the core of her message is important not only for women but also for men. When it comes to your home life, career and finances, it is very important that your spouse is aggressively and deeply supportive of your decisions and thoughts. It is also important that your husband is willing and able to meet you halfway.

To put it in other words, the single most important money decision that you will ever make is your husband.

Your Husband Can Impact Your Career

Though you marry your husband because you love him, it is also important to take into account how he may impact your work life. According to a recent Washington University study, the person you choose as your life partner can help you become successful in your career.

One of the co-authors of the study, Brittany Solomon, said that they found that the personality traits of marriage partners can actually influence each of the partners' individual outcomes.

The study, which was published Psychological Science, found that an individual's work success does not solely depend on her own personality. The personality of a spouse also affects whether we find success or failure in the work place.

The five-year study examined 5,000 married people ranging in age from 19 to 89 years. Roughly three quarters of the sample included homes in which both spouses were employed. The researchers administered psychological tests to assess the participants in five broad personality areas: extraversion, openness, neuroticism, conscientiousness and agreeableness.

The researchers went further, tracking the on-the-job performance of employed spouses by using yearly surveys to measure occupational success. Additionally, each worker was asked to provide self-reports about salary increases, job satisfaction and the chances of earning a promotion.

While previous studies have also shown that it's important to get married to a husband who ranks highly in agreeableness, this research showed that female workers who had the highest occupational success had partners who ranked highly for conscientiousness.

Conscientiousness is determined by the tendency to be dependable and organised. Conscientious people also practice self-discipline and strive for achievement. Subsequently they prefer to work on planned activities rather than spontaneous events and also behave dutifully.

3 Ways a Conscientious Husband Contributes to Your Success

According to the research, conscientious partners promote career success irrespective of whether both the partners are working or not. The study also concluded that a conscientious partner is important for both women and men. The study authors discovered that there are three main ways a conscientious person can support the career of a spouse.

Completing daily tasks

The conscientious partner performs household chores, shops for groceries, pays bills and even cares for children. This way, the working spouse is freed to complete work outside home.

Keeping your life running smoothly

The conscientious partner promotes a healthy work-life balance and reduces overall stress, helping the other to advance a career.

Promoting healthy habits

A working partner learns and practices some good habits, such as reliability and diligence, both of which improve career success.

Your Husband Could Contribute Precious Insights

Husbands can also provide insights into your work life that you may not have otherwise had. Dennis J. O'Neil, an executive coach, describes once having a client who asked him to mail a written assessment report to his home rather than to his office. After reading the report, the client's wife told him, 'Your Company used a lot of money on this report, but it's exactly what I've been telling you.' His partner's insight was as helpful as that of a business coach!

Your husband's involvement and support can do more than just support your job. Through his different perspective and your own thoughtful analysis, you can distinguish yourself at the workplace, learning new behaviours and even becoming significantly happier and more successful.

Your Husband Can Also Hurt Your Career

A caring husband can be an important part of having a robust career, but it doesn't necessarily mean that having a conscientious spouse will keep your career from failure. The personality of your partner can drastically affect your career, both positively and negatively, according to University of North Carolina professor, Christopher Hall.

The perfect relationship is one where both partners offer non-judgmental, caring and partner-focused encouragement. These factors make it possible for the partners to take risks in their careers. However, though partners may feel that they are supporting each other, according to Hall, sometimes partners only want the other person to make a decision that will serve their own interest. Your partner may be knowingly or unknowingly using you for personal gain.

Your Husband Will Impact Your Reputation

Do you realise that what your husband says about you to his friends and relatives can affect your reputation? Some men repeatedly belittle their wives in front of other people, and this can lead people to disrespect them. Although it is your responsibility to behave in a manner that is respectable, it is also your husband's responsibility to talk about you in a way which preserves and also builds your reputation. You do not want him to reveal your faults and shortcomings to the whole world.

This doesn't mean that your husband should religiously hide your sins from people who ought to know them. However he does need to be very careful and respectful when speaking about you wherever possible.

Will the man you consider to be your husband tear down your reputation or build it up? Will he teach your kids to respect you, or will he teach your own family to belittle you? Will the man tell everyone about your failings who cares to listen to him, or will he, out of love, conceal them from the world but help you privately to fight them?

Your Husband Will Affect Your Health

A pestering, nagging and quick-tempered husband is too dangerous to your health. Many women I know who got married to this kind of man are ready to live on a roof just to get a semblance of mental peace.

Will the man you are considering marrying mentally wear you down by constant pestering and nagging, or will he prevent frustration as much as possible by sharing his opinions and allowing you to lead at times? Is he going to respect you and your judgment?

For example, will he support you to lose weight by encouraging you to eat healthy meals and exercise, or will he constantly complain about your weight and embarrass you publicly?

Your Husband Will Impact Your Other Relationships

Though you are the one who will live with this man, it is also important to take into account what those who are close to you think of your future husband. What, for instance, is your mother going to think of your man? Does he respect your parents? Is your man happy to have your parents as the grandparents of your children? Although you need to carve your own life and leave your parents, it is still important that you take their advice into consideration since they will also be affected by your choice.

How will your choice of a husband affect your male mentors and friends? Will your future partner allow you to continue your relationships with your older mentors, or will he complain about privacy? Will he allow you to visit your church members and other friends?

Your Husband Will Affect Your Spiritual Life

If you are a firm believer in any religion, it is important that the person you choose to be your husband is also a believer. If he is not, it would be a lot wiser to drop him. Knowing that he will not support or allow you to continue to pursue your faith, you don't have to start a relationship with him. You need to decide whether you are going to stay true to your religion or if you want to be falsely nice.

In Summary: What We Can Learn from the Study

A husband can genuinely help advance your career, doing more than just encouraging you to apply for a new job or ask for a raise. Work success depends a lot on having a husband who makes your life outside of work run smoothly and supports your career goals.

If you are a woman aged over 35 years and you are ambitious about your career endeavours, you must give serious thought to the conscientiousness of your potential mate. The person you choose to marry will affect you in many ways, and this also includes your work life. Be very choosy about the man you marry, especially if you want to develop your career.

The most important lesson to learn from this research is that we should know how our partners' personality will affect us. Simply taking note of the behaviours and characteristics that may help or hinder us can aid us in finding someone who can help us meet our goals.

For more information about how to go about getting the man of your dream, go to www.TheLoveListBook.com to download a free workbook.

CHAPTER 4

Know What You Don't Want

Dating is a great learning experience. The search for Prince Charming can be a little frustrating, and sometimes you may want to overlook some negative qualities just so that you can finally conclude the search. However as someone who has dated several kinds of men, trust me when I tell you that most of these types are not worth sharing a house with.

There are some men you shouldn't touch with a ten-inch pole. Read on to learn the types of men you should never consider putting up with.

1. The Jekyll-And-Hyde Drunk

When you first meet this man, you have the feeling that you are the luckiest girl because you have found a man who is not only smart and creative but also interesting. He seems to have the best behaviour. Since his former friends have told him that his drinking is sometimes problematic, he minimises his drinking when he's around you. However once he gets somewhere he feels comfortable, he gets incredibly inebriated because he wants to have fun just like everyone else. And if you catch him at it, that's when you see the monster in him. Suddenly you see the man spewing all manner of hateful and nasty things. He doesn't look like the gentleman you have been going out with. He is like a petulant child who needs babysitting and his behaviours border on the dangerous and erratic. When he is drunk, this kind of man easily gets into fights with others and won't listen to anyone. You find it both frustrating and confusing since the guy is cool and normal when he's sober but a beast when he's drunk. In most cases, these drastically opposing types of behavior are indicative of some serious underlying issues, which he has yet to deal with. Although you may want to try and fix this kind of a person, it is simply not worth your patience and sanity. Let him deal with his own problems.

2. The Alcoholic

This kind of a man should not be confused with the Jekyll-and-Hyde Drunk. Instead the alcoholic man mostly keeps it together and will rarely act irrationally, even when intoxicated. The reason is because the alcoholic is constantly self-medicating. His issues come to life not when he's inebriated but rather when he's sober, which is why he would rather block out and consequently numb anything resembling feelings. Thus you are left wondering if there will be any day that you will see him sober. You may even fail to take note of the drinking as it is a normal thing for him. He won't drive much and will always prefer to end the day at his home so he can take one more cocktail. Because such kinds of people rarely have clear heads, you will never be really sure about the kind of person he is. For him, nothing will ever get too personal, real or deep. Even if you try to come up with sober activities, he won't seem very interested in participating. He won't engage with you during the day if he's sober, preferring instead to do something while in the comfort of his drink.

3. The Cheater or Manipulator

You probably got hooked on this guy while he was in another relationship. He will insist that things between his partner and him are so bad and that they are likely to break up. You know that hanging out with him while he is still seeing another person is wrong and you don't want to do it, but you are unable to push him away. Once this guy hooks up with you, you might then think that you are the perfect person for him. You might even feel that he and his ex aren't really meant for each other. The universe attracted you two together, and therefore your relationship with him is meant to be. Wake up from your slumber! Chances are that this kind of man will cheat on you as well. Why do you expect that he will act differently toward you than he would have with other girls? This is the kind of person that identifies what he wants and does not hesitate to go after it, no matter the consequences. To him, right or wrong do not mean a thing and neither do his relationships. The only thing he cares about is pleasure and personal gain. Should you catch him, he is always armed with loads of excuses to give. It is possible that this kind of person also cheats in life and not just with women. He probably also cheats on tests or even steals ideas from other people and uses them to get ahead at the workplace. He is calculating and very smart, and he is a smooth talker who charms his way to anything that he wants. If you notice your man constantly making excuses for the wrong behaviours, you need to look for a new one.

4. The Controller

From what you are wear to the amount of makeup that you have on, from what you eat to how you do your hair, this is the kind of guy that will always make you feel bad for everything. He will also belittle your intelligence and question any idea that you bring to the table. He will rarely support what you do, and instead he will regularly and snidely critique it. This kind of a husband gets jealous all the time, and he wants to know where you are as well as what you are doing. He might also be a misogynist, but do not expect that he will ever admit it. The worst form of the Controller is an abusive person. Although it's obvious that you should give this type of guy a wide berth, some women get too deeply attached to them before they even realise that the guy is capable of committing such atrocities. However the truth is that you can recognise this type of a man long before you get into a deep relationship with him. Pay attention to the manner he treats other people. Does he appear mean to customer service reps or waiters? Does he seem to be always criticising everyone around him? If the answer is yes, then you are staring right at a Controller type of a guy.

5. The Commitment-Phobe

Though his behaviour may not be as egregious as the others', this man will still ruin you emotionally. Usually this guy has it all together. Not only is he mature, but he's also wise. He treats you very well and generally likes to spend time with you. He leaves you craving more. However he only wants to enjoy the current moment with you and you won't hear him talk seriously of marriage or moving in with you, no matter the length of your relationship. This sort of a guy likes simply cruising along. He wants to have a person that he spends time with when he wants, but apart from that your lives are very much separate. If you have a lot of patience and can wait for him maybe forever to propose, then by all means be with this man. Perhaps if you don't want commitment yourself, he could be a perfect match for you. However for anyone else, do avoid this guy as much as you can.

6. Mr. Gadget

This type of a man is always flaunting the latest big boy toys. He sports the latest phone, the newest Harley and the hottest luxury car or a high-speedboat. Put differently, this sort of man invests in expensive material things to keep him busy. He is a grown-up child who simply cannot resist the latest plaything, and this means he simply cannot keep his attention on you. Whether he just wants to impress his friends or he buys the latest gadgets to feed his own ego, this is a guy who cares more for stuff than for human beings. You can be sure that if an upgraded gadget hits the market, you will be obsolete to him.

7. The Mama's Boy

This kind of a man probably still puts up with his parents, enabling his mom to launder clothes for him, cook meals and make his bed. But the truth is that when a grown-up man enjoys being constantly waited on by his mother, there is trouble. A Mama's Boy usually expects his girlfriend to endlessly cater to him, and he never understands why doing so would be a problem. Rather than having to raise a grown-up man, most women just leave the parenting bit to his mother.

8. The Roving-Eye Guy

When you are seated with this guy, you realise that he is constantly gazing at every female but you. He will ogle the barista, his buddy's wife, the woman at the customer service desk at a grocery store and just about anyone wearing a miniskirt. In so doing, he makes you feel both inferior and unattractive. Although men are naturally inclined to admire attractive women, recognising beauty is very different from rubbernecking. Thus you will find yourself constantly competing for his attention. If you realise that your man's inappropriate gestures, looks, comments, smarmy smile and eager interest in other ladies are distracting from your relationship, you need to pick up and move along. Your man needs to treat you as though you are the only lady in the room.

9. The 'My Way Or The Highway' Man

Selfish people can't compromise or handle sacrifice, two very important elements that are vital to happy marriages. This kind of man believes his desires and needs are more important than yours. He is therefore the person who makes all decisions. He is not for a legitimate partnership but just wants a woman to keep him company and to act as both admirer and therapist.

10. The Overly Romantic

This type of husband will consistently ignore any signs of an unhappy relationship. While romance is definitely an important ingredient for a happy marriage, it won't keep a relationship alive on its own. Even if a couple is constantly engaging in fights, the overly romantic man will bear the brunt of unhappiness since he is convinced he is with the perfect soul mate.

Mistakes to Avoid When Searching for a Husband

The relationship you choose to be in is what eventually determines the happiness you have. If you are a Single Sally, you will notice that married couples are having fun. According to research, married people are generally happier than singles.

http://www.dailymail.co.uk/

However not all married couples are happy. Some are downright miserable, usually because they chose wrong partners to marry. Choosing a man that you will live with for the rest of your life is no simple task, and most women don't realise how important the decision is. The majority of women don't think they will end up divorcing their husbands. Research shows that 86 percent of young people expect their future marriages to last forever. http://www. huffingtonpost.com/ Aug 17, 2012

However when you are picking a life partner, there are a lot of details that you are cementing in just one decision, and it can be very difficult to get all of it right. You are choosing several things, including a father for your children, a role model for your children, your career therapist, your friend, your fellow retiree and travel companion. That's a lot of stuff to put on one person, and so you need to be very careful not to make any mistakes in your choice.

HERE ARE THE MISTAKES TO AVOID WHEN CHOOSING A MARRIAGE PARTNER.

Marrying someone that you expect to change

This is a classic mistake that women make when choosing someone to marry. The golden rule is that if you are not happy with a man the way he is now, do not get married. You can actually expect your man to change after you marry him…. for the worse! Therefore when it comes to the man's character, spirituality, personal hygiene, character, personal habits and communication skills, ensure that you can put up with them as they are now.

Marrying under societal pressure

A lot of women, who reach a certain age of singleness, feel pressured to settle down with a man and start their own family. However the choice of the person to marry is too serious to be left to your mother, relatives or society at large. Do not marry someone you aren't sure about just because you think it's the right decision. Make sure you love the person, and don't get married because of societal pressure. Before you decide on the person to settle down with, make sure that you are emotionally in the perfect place, focusing on character rather than chemistry. Although chemistry ignites the relationship's fire, it is good character that will keep the fire burning. Most women get married because they are in love. Even if it is obvious that you are attracted to the man, still take your time to check out his character. Four character traits that you want to check out for are humility, kindness, responsibility and happiness. Is it more important to him to do the right thing than to pursue his own comfort? Does your man enjoy pleasing other people? Does he give charity or do volunteer work? Can you rely on this man to do what he says he is going to do? Does he enjoy life? Does he like himself? Do you want to be like this person? Are you comfortable having kids with him? Would you like your children to become like him? Examining your answers to these questions will help you assess your man's character and whether you're comfortable to spend your life with him, chemistry or not.

Marrying someone despite the fact that his family doesn't like you

How does his family treat you? Do they like you? Do his family members welcome you into their family? Although it doesn't appear like an important thing when you first begin dating, getting along well with his family is something that you need to consider when you want to settle down with him. If you are marrying in a culture where you and your husband will move in with his family, it is especially important that you enjoy a cordial relationship with them. Otherwise you may be facing a lot of tension. Even if your partner gives you a lot of support, it is still important to live in an environment that is friendly and which feels like a home to you.

Marrying to escape unhappiness and personal problems

If you are single and unhappy, you will probably end up married and unhappy, too. Marriages don't fix personal, emotional and psychological problems. In fact marriages are more likely to compound these problems. If you feel unhappy with your life and yourself, take time to fix it now while still single. You will feel better, and even your husband will thank you for that.

Marrying a man with whom you don't have a deep, emotional connection

Do you admire and respect this man? Having a deep, emotional connection does not mean simply being impressed by the man. You may be impressed by a Mercedes that he owns, but you cannot respect a person simply because he owns a Mercedes. Instead his qualities of determination, loyalty and creativity should impress you. Also you need to ask yourself if you trust the person. Is he emotionally stable? Do you feel that you can rely on him?

Why We Marry the Wrong Husbands

We cannot put up with being single

You will never be in the right frame of mind to pick a man rationally when you cannot put up with being single. It is important that you are utterly at peace with the possibility of spending many years single to have a real chance at having a good relationship. It is better to be single and happy than to be married and unhappy. Unfortunately, after attaining a certain age, singleness is made dangerously unpleasant by society. But it is still very possible to find love beyond the age of 35. The most important thing is not just to get married but to do so to a person whom you will love and cherish and with whom you will bring up good children.

We do not understand the men we marry

Marrying someone you barely understand is the first sin that we can make when it comes to marriage. We believe that after visiting their families and knowing where the man studied, we know them. We look at photos and meet their friends. But we often stop there as we fallaciously think we have done our homework.

However this is just like a novice pilot who assumes that just because he can send a paper plane around the room successfully, he can fly. In order to fully understand your man, you need to put him through a detailed psychological questionnaire and have him assessed by a team of psychologists. It might sound like a joke now, but by the year 2100, this will be the norm. You need to know the intimate functioning behind the man that you are planning to marry. You particularly need to know their attitudes and stance on humiliation, authority, sexual intimacy, introspection, money, children, fidelity, ageing and lots of other things. You won't find this knowledge through a standard chat. It requires years of digging up. Without this detailed analysis, we are often led astray by the appearance of the man we want to spend the whole of our lives with. Although there is a lot of information that can be gleaned from his eyes, his smiles, the distribution of his freckles, the shape of his forehead and his nose, this is as wise as looking at his photo and marrying him on the basis of these things alone.

We don't understand exactly what we want

When we are looking for a partner for the first time, our requirements for them can be a little vague. Most of us will say we want someone attractive and kind or someone who is up for adventure. Wanting these things is not wrong, but the problem is that these desires are not remotely helpful for determining exactly what we are going to need for us to be happy in marriage. To this end, you need to have a specific picture of the man that you want to marry. Having several qualities you are looking for means you will not just fall for him because he is attractive.

Starting Your Love List Using Your Previous Relationships

Many of us have had past relationships and if you haven't then perhaps you should skip this chapter. However for those of you who have had previous relationships, start to think about all the things your ex-partner did that annoyed you. Though no one is perfect and you won't be able to find Mr. Perfect, you will find Mr. Right. Mr. Right is the one that will accept your warts and look over your faults and love you for who you are. After all your faults make up part of you, as well, don't they? Just the same way he will accept you, there are things about him that will annoy you, but you need to make a conscious decision to decide if you will be able put up with those annoying things for the rest of your life. By having failed relationships, you will have learned about the things you are not willing to accept. Having these non-negotiables is totally fine and gives you a reference where your starting point will be.

Exercise One: Can't Stands

Starting a relationship is far easier than breaking one up. Once we enter into a relationship, we create soul ties. We start to memorise dates, things our partner said to us, little nicknames and so many other things. Then when it comes to the not-so-nice things, we start hurting and getting upset and angry. Remembering these things from your past relationship, these are the things that now you need to write down in the column on your Love List that says 'Can't stand.' Think of the emotions that came with that thing you were thinking of; how did it make you feel? Annoyed, hurt, in pain, angry, hateful, guilty? On a scale of 1 to10 with 10 being the highest, how did those possible 'Can't Stand' qualities in your old relationships make you feel? If you were in the 7-10 range, then you definitely should write those qualities down in the 'Can't Stand 'column.

Exercise Two: Must Haves

Once you have gotten through all your negative feelings - this is the nicer section! - do exactly the same thing as you did in Exercise One: reflect on your previous relationships. But this time relax, close your eyes and think of all the good things your ex-partner did for you, all the things he said and did that made you feel loved, wanted and special. Maybe you went out on a date to somewhere you had always wanted to go, or maybe you went on holiday and he treated you like a princess. How did he make you feel?

As you do these exercises notice your body language? Think about your feelings, where these feelings come from and where they go to and where they sit on a scale of 1 to10. Write down these good things on the Love List too because you know what makes you feel good and there is no point being in a relationship where the other person doesn't make you feel good.

After all the best part of a relationship is when you both know how to make each other feel like they are the only person in the world. We humans were designed to be with someone else. We are social creatures, and when we are with a partner we are more balanced and able to totally fulfil our purpose. Though I do not mean that we need someone to validate us but in the beginning of time this is how it was.

After working through these two exercises, you should have a pretty good idea of what you absolutely can't stand in your life partner and what you would love to have. But basing your entire Love List on previous relationships would be pretty limiting. After all you are no longer with those ex-partners and probably for a good reason. From here on in, we're going to focus on what you do want, what you haven't had yet in a partner but ultimately what you know you can't live without.

CHAPTER 5

Decide What You Do Want

Know What You Want

As we've explored throughout the previous chapters, knowing exactly what it is you are looking for in a partner allows to really go to work and make this relationship real. But a lot of what we've explored so far has been what you don't want. Though learning from your past experiences and being sure of what you don't want is important, now let's be a little more proactive and decide what you do want.

Be definite and purposeful about everything you want in life, not just in a lifetime partner. When you start to administer this process of thinking to other areas of your life, you will see how this works and how easy it actually is to have the things you want.

We All Have a Dream Partner

Your ideal partner may be in your head, but you can make him come to you in reality. Get him out of your head and into your life. Didn't Michael Jackson sing a song similar to that? Well it's true. However whatever you do, ensure you discuss your Love List with selected people as not everyone will share the same thoughts as you. Just today I was going to the dry cleaners to get my dress and coat cleaned, and on the way I met Sharlette and Anthony. We somehow started talking about my book, but they both had different views about Love Lists. Sharlette agreed with me that we women should have Love Lists whilst Anthony was deadset against it, saying that we women are limiting ourselves by writing a List.

We had a nice little debate; he gave me his perspective, thoughts and values, though we didn't agree. Anthony believes that we women should not limit ourselves by writing a specific Love List, thinking we are limiting ourselves while our knight in shining armour could come disguised as something we don't expect. Meanwhile Sharlette totally agrees we should have a Love List.

Having this debate with Anthony reminded me of my many conversations with Matthew, someone who also thinks that I should dump my Love List. But you know that is never going to happen, don't you, Matthew?

Let me tell you something. If you believe you can have the man in your head, then you surely can. You only have to stay with your process and believe in yourself.

Think About Him Every Day

Oh my goodness, this is one of the best parts for me! I really enjoy doing this, especially when I have to take public transport. I get more time to speak to him like he is already there. I tell him what my day is going to be like, and when I get home I tell him what I did, how my day went, what good deals I made, if anyone upset me. But most of all I love to tell him how much I love him. The feeling that comes over me is a feeling of peace, love, understanding and togetherness.

Exercise Three: Imagine Your Perfect Day Together

For a third exercise designed to help you really develop your Love List and eventually visualise your future partner, write down a whole day spent with your partner. If you're already in a relationship, you can visualise an ideal day with your partner. If you're still looking, imagine the perfect day with your future spouse. Make it a day that belongs to you both. Go out do something special, and write it all down. If you don't know where to start, then just start from the first thing you do in the morning. Perhaps you wake up at 7 AM, go to bathroom, take a shower, and at 7:30 AM prepare breakfast. After breakfast you discuss what both will have for our picnic lunch. We talk about the fillings we want in our sandwiches, what kind of drinks we are going to bring with us and so on. This is just a brief example.

You must make your story come to life. If you are talking about food, tell us what the food smells like. Remember that you don't have to see a KFC to know it is there; it is their sales point. You smell their chicken cooking first, long before you can see them. Do you think this is by accident? How many times have you been down a high street and you smelt the cooking of Kentucky Fried Chicken? Their shops are purposely designed so that the smell can drift down the road.

This is how you need to make your story sound, look, and smell, using all the senses. When you describe something you should:

- Communicate with him regularly

- Speak him into existence

- Commit him to paper and memory

Visualisation is an important tool for helping you to achieve your goals. If this exercise resonated with you, we work more with vision boards and visualisation in Chapter 6.

CHAPTER 6

When to compromise

It's ok to change your mind

We are all at different places in our lives, so we shouldn't look at what others are doing or where they are in their love lives as a comparison. You are an individual, and you are unique; your circumstances will therefore also be unique. I have six sisters, and if we all cooked a pot of pasta, there would be seven different textures because we are different and unique and do the same things different. Don't judge your relationship based on those of others.

You will find that as you grow and evolve, so will your needs and wants. It is ok for you to change your mind about things, including things about your relationship desires. I used to be into the property industry in a big way, so one of the things that I needed was someone that could help me repair and decorate my properties. So I put on my List that I needed a builder. However some years went by and I no longer spend time decorating or repairing my properties myself. Instead I hire people to do it, so I changed the requirements on my List. I no longer need a builder; I want something else.

You don't need to be rigid with your List. Spend time reviewing, evaluating and updating your List over time. It is your life, and you are in charge of creating your destiny.

If you have your essential qualities on your List in order of importance, you will know exactly what you can compromise on in a partner. Have special headings to make it easy to put things on your List, and don't be afraid to play with words and change them around. I often revise my List, but I always have a reason why I want a certain thing.

Be Sure About the Changes You Make on Your List

No one can really be 100 percent sure about what they want, but you can have a pretty good idea. Because we are humans, our wants and needs will change on a regular basis. All you have to do is think about yourself this time last year or the year before, and you will notice the things that have changed in your life since then. Maybe you have changed your car, your job, your bedroom decor or even your accommodation.

Change is inevitable, and we shouldn't resist it. Without change we would be stagnant, inactive, motionless and not moving forward. Have you smelt stagnant water? Wooo! It actually stinks really badly. You don't want to be caught in life's stagnant, dirty water because your life will surely smell rotten to the core, and let's face it, that would not be a pretty sight.

When doing our spring cleaning we decide when it needs to be done, prepare our minds and put time aside so that we can do it. Cleaning up your Love List is no different. Make special time to clean your List up. This is your life we are talking about, and how many lives do you have? My sister always tells me that we are 'dead a lot longer than we're alive', so whilst we are here on this earth we need to make the most of our time. Revisit your List and delete, amend or add things as needed.

We Evolve Daily

Every single day is a new day, and along with each new day comes new changes, challenges, obstacles and, of course, opportunities. How we deal with these daily changes is definitely up to us, so try to stay as positive as possible. Just the same way as snakes shed their skin so we should shed the old scales from our bodies daily and move into fresh, new exciting things.

I know that this all sounds like I am living in a fairy land, but how we approach situations lies with us. We are the masters of our own destinies, and though we cannot stop things that happen around us, we can change how we deal with them.

If you are not already, you will soon evolve into a beautiful butterfly. You are being crystalised right now, and it is only a matter of time before you fly and become free.

As humans, some of us understandably are afraid to evolve. Just remember that evolving is a part of your life's journey and there is nothing you can do to change it. Some people go and have cosmetic surgery regain their youth instead of embracing their age and flying like a butterfly. Having said that, I do use facial makeup to help me evolve and develop.

Your Have Needs

Just the same way you have evolved and accepted the changes that come about in your life, so do your needs evolve and change.

Don't be afraid to change your mind and prioritise your needs. Remember that you are in charge.

CHAPTER 7

Picture the Man You Want

Throughout this book, you have been working on developing your Love List. You know what you don't want, you've determined what you do want, and you've worked a small bit on visualising your life with your ideal partner. Now it's time to make your Love List more than just a list of qualities.

Whether or not we realise it, not many of us women have a mental picture of the husband that we would like to marry. When we go out to a party, we will meet people who interest us and people who don't. We naturally categorise men by comparing them with the mental picture we have. The mental picture of the man you want to marry is usually shaped right from your childhood and through your upbringing and is influenced by the society, culture and environment we live in.

A mental picture of the man that you would like to marry is important in clarifying the specific type of partner that you want to spend the rest of your life with and is crucial in committing your Love List to paper. Throughout this chapter, we will work on practicing visualisation and helping you take your Love List to the next level.

Below are the ten points that you need to consider when conjuring up the image of the right partner for you.

1. Personality

There are so many personalities out there, which is why picturing the man with the perfect personality for you is a complicated process. There are things that you must be able to compromise on as no one is perfect, but this does not mean that you should not know and be solid in your vision of the man you want to end up with.

To help you explore the personality of your ideal partner, pose these questions to yourself:

• Would you want a calm, talkative, outgoing or shy guy?

• Would you want to be with a man who is soft and rarely gets angry or would you prefer a brutally honest and direct man?

• Do you want a calm and easy going man or a husband who is full of energy and logical?

- Do you want a calm and serious guy, or a funny and expressive one?

- Do you like a strong and independent person, or a husband who allows you to decide things?

2. Level Intelligence

No woman would be happy to marry a man who is not intelligent. We all need to be with people who can help us solve our problems and people who are resourceful to us in one way or another. Our partner may have an inferior education in comparison with ours, but that is not to say they are stupid. Ultimately consider the perfect partner to be someone of a similar level of intelligence as yourself. If the intelligence gap between you and the man you want to marry is too big, there will be problems in communication.

When visualising your ideal partner, it is very important to consider the level of intelligence between you two. If you want to be the dominant force in the relationship, you may settle for someone who is less intelligent than you. The majority however probably would love to marry a man we can depend on, which means they want to be with someone who is highly intelligent and on a close level of intelligence with ourselves. Decide on the kind of man you want and factor this in your mental image.

3. Physical Appearance

Our ideas of men's physical appearance are influenced by magazines, TV programmes and other mass media, as well as the society that we all live in. Although physical appearance should never rank above character when deciding on the love of your life, you still need to consider if your ideal partner meets your personal taste. You will have to consider your preferences like height, dressing style, hairstyle, and cleanliness as well as how he carries himself.

As you would expect, the importance that women place on physical appearance in a spouse varies. Some women love a tall and strong guy while others would be happy with any man that loves them. Physical appearance is subjective. Just decide on who you want based on appearance, and create a mental picture of him.

4. Ambition

Another important thing to consider when picturing your ideal man is ambition. If you and your man are going to succeed, it is very important that you have identical levels of ambition. Ambition will inform how you run the family. If you marry a highly ambitious man, chances are that he will spend a big chunk of his time at the workplace and at the expense of his family. If you do not also have this level of ambition, you won't understand him, and this can lead to fractions in the marriage. You might feel unloved if your husband is away most times.

On the flipside, if you marry a husband who is less ambitious than yourself, chances are that he might feel inferior. Therefore it is important that when visualising the man to marry, you also consider how ambitious or not ambitious you want your man to be. If you share the same ambitions with your would-be-husband, you are likely to be more in-tune with each other. If both of you dream of having a big house, regular holidays and plenty of cars, both of you have to work hard to achieve this. But if you do not share the same wants and needs, whatever they may be, be ready for conflict and frustrations.

5. Chemistry

Chemistry plays an important role in bringing two people together. It is what makes two people feel comfortable with one another, talk for hours, enjoy each other and fall for each other. Good chemistry is very important in keeping you and your future husband together.

Chemistry, however, is not necessarily about physical appearance but about personality. You want to easily connect with this person from the first time that you see him. Even if he is handsome, you won't love him if there is no chemistry between you. Both physical appearance and attraction are things that fade with time. When they are no longer there, it is the chemistry that will be keeping you together.

6. Spirituality

Experts point out that the success of a marriage is very much linked to the mutual commitment to religion. http://www.theguardian.com.

It is very important that the man in your mental picture has the same religious background as you. This not only strongly ties you together with your partner but also ties you strongly to your religious beliefs. If you and your partner don't have the same beliefs, you will constantly be arguing with each other.

Mutual spirituality doesn't just imply that the two of you should subscribe to the same religion. It has more to do with how much you two are going to live a spiritual life together. If you are the kind that prays often, will you be expecting your partner to also pray? If your relationship with God is important to you, will you put up with a man who doesn't really care about God? If you have a deep relationship with God, it is likely that you will want a partner who has similar affection for God.

Spirituality is a very important part of marriage. The two of you need to be of the same spiritual orientation and beliefs. If for instance there is a problem in the house and you believe you need to pray so for God's intervention, your husband must be able to share in this belief. Otherwise there will be serious problems in your marriage.

7. Character

When picturing the man you want, you need to be very clear regarding the character that you want him to display. You want someone you can trust and who is honest, full of joy, stable and humble. You want to marry a man you will be proud to be the father of your children. If you catch your man lying or cheating, you want to seriously think about your relationship. One of the cornerstones of a relationship is honesty. Do not put your future and the future of your children in the hands of a man you have caught cheating.

Other traits that you want your man to have are emotional balance, anger control and humility. It is very important that you think of the characteristics that you want your future husband to have. You should not marry an irascible man that can't control his anger in front of children. In the same way, you should not put up with an arrogant husband. The character is very important because this is the man you are going to live with for the rest of your life.

8. Creativity

This has more to do with balance. There are many men out there who are great businessmen and leaders but who just can't spend their time at home with family. These men would rather be alone in their own space, and you will most likely be frustrated by someone who is good at one thing and terrible at the other. This is why you need an all-around creative person.

9. Parenting

Being married means that you are definitely on your way to becoming a parent. The man you marry will also be the father of your children. He should have the parenting ideals that you want as well. The man you have at the back of your mind should be a great father and a role model to your kids. Parenting is a key aspect of a strong marriage, and the two of you must be in sync in the raising of your kids. Your children are likely to be the centre of both of your lives. The way that the two of you expect to live as parents as well as a loving couple is critical to an everlasting marriage.

10. Being Real

It is common for women to try to be someone other than who they actually are when trying to catch the attention of a man. If for example you come from a rich family and you are in love with a man from a less affluent background, are you genuine when you say that you can leave behind all the glamour and settle with this man?

The Love List, Sonia Poléon

Deep down in your heart, you know that you probably can't leave such a life, but you keep pretending that you will. This is self-denial, and it is not really you. Such stories of a rich girl falling for a poor guy are for the movies. They don't work in real life. After getting married and facing hard times financially, you will see the reality of living in squalor.

What makes a marriage great are the two REAL people that form it. These are people who aren't hiding anything or any feelings. You are being real when you are not faking anything in order to be loved. Being real means loving each other as you both are. If early on you pretend that you love something when you don't, you will be very unhappy later in the marriage. A real matrimonial union is built on emotional stability found inside each partner. Stability is brought about by brutal honesty from you without attempting to fake or hide anything.

Is there anything you are faking right now in a relationship? Do you pretend that everything is fine when in actual fact you hate what he is doing? Are you faking happiness?

No relationship is faultless, and every relationship requires a bit of compromising and adjusting.

How to Visualise the Man of Your Dreams

Visualisation is a very good tool for bringing to reality your dreams and goals. By picturing the man you want, you will be able to have a clearer picture of the man that you are looking for. Knowing clearly what you are after, it becomes easier to focus.

Below are 10 tips to maximise the effectiveness of visualisation so as to attract the perfect mate.

1. Be Consistent

Only occasionally visualising your man is not effective. Rather you need to be consistent and picture him on a daily basis. You need just a few minutes every day. This creates a solid picture of the type of man you are looking for.

2. Inject Emotion

You need to feel the emotions you would experience if you were with the man of your dreams. Would you feel joyful, excited, peaceful and secure? Mix whatever feelings you associate with a happy marriage when you practice your visualisation.

3. Focus on What You Want

When visualising, focus solely on the exact kind of man that you want to spend your life with. Keep yourself positive. You will notice that you always have a beaming smile when visualising, especially if you are genuinely focused on the image of the man you desire and like the experience you see in your mind.

4. Have all your senses involved into your visualisation

Remember to be as detailed as possible. Imagine going to a destination you have always dreamed of with your husband. Picture him carrying you on his back as you play around in the jungle. How does it feel? What sounds do you hear? These thoughts help make your goal real. You believe more in being able to find that man. The more belief you have, the more successful you will be.

5. Create a dream notebook or a vision board

Cut some pictures of couples embracing, holding hands, and kissing or doing things together. Take a few minutes every day to look at these images. You may also paste a picture of a couple on the mirror on your bathroom or on your desk. The point is to be able to see this picture every day so it helps you focus on the man you want.

6. Put images, hearts or any love symbols you like throughout your house

Collect items that represent love, and enjoyably decorate your home with them. Every time you see these items, you will be immediately reminded of your goal which is to attract a good man to marry you.

7. Reorganise Your Bedroom

As you visualise the right man coming into your life, it is important that you free up some space in your bedroom for him. Make space for his clothes and visualise his clothing in those spaces. Even go as far as freeing up the spaces on the dresser or the night stand for your new love to put a few things. You may even want to hire a Feng Shui consultant to ensure that your bedroom is organised and primed to welcome home your new love.

8. Be happy for others

If a friend or a person you know finds love, congratulate them. Also enjoy anniversaries and weddings. Picture yourself being congratulated when you are a couple.

9. Practice patience

In most cases, what you want also wants you. It is important that you are truly open and available to new love. Make sure that you are primed and ready for a new and lasting relationship. Have all the conflicts in your mind cleared, and clear anything that may hinder your eagerness for a relationship. After that, be persistent in your visualisation efforts and patient in your practice.

10. Have Faith

Getting the man of your dream is not something that you can rush. Feelings of urgency and desperation rarely help in realising your goal. Relax, have fun and believe that it's possible to achieve your goal.

If you practice visualisation correctly and regularly, you will realise that not only is it fun but is also something that can actually help attract a man into your life. The key is to get creative and try out many different visualisation variations. This will prevent boredom and at the same time create excitement. Before you know it, your vision will become a reality.

Using Vision Boards to Picture your Dream Husband

Vision boards are very good tools you can use to visualise and create a life that you want. It could be that you want the perfect job, a good home or a good man to marry. Since you still don't have a soul mate, you can take advantage of vision boards to attract the man you want to spend your life with forever.

Use the tips below to get started:

Appearance

Appearance may not rank above the character of a person in importance, but many people are still attracted to what they see. In fact what people find on the outside is what they are likely to get inside. It is possible to find someone with good character who is still attractive.

So which physical features are most attractive to you? Write them down in a list as follows:

- Hair- style, length, colour

- Body- muscular or fit

- Height- short, tall, standard

Having a mental image of your ideal husband enables you to easily find pictures of similar men, which you will then paste onto your board. What you want to attract in a romantic partner also needs to be reflected on your board. Thus your board needs to have the picture of that man you would term as an ideal mate.

Personality

At this point, you have a clear mental image of your future husband in your mind. But what about his character? How does he behave? What are examples of words you would use to describe your man? They might include the following:

- Shy

- Friendly

Genuine

- Sincere

- Confident

- Warm

- Bubbly

- Charismatic

- Outgoing

- Funny

- Caring

- Serious

- Temperament

Temperament describes the way that a person reacts when upset. Do you want to end up with a man who exhibits passion in his opinions or convictions? Do you want a man who fights for what he wants? Or do you want a rather subdued man, someone who displays calmness even in the face of challenge?

Goals and Aspirations

As you look for and visualise that special someone, you will probably be more concerned about future goals. Still, before you get too deeply involved with this man, it is important that you check with him to ensure that your goals dovetail with his.

This also means that you need to have your life goals written on your vision board as well. Your goals might include:

- Children

- Marriage

- Buying a home

- Traveling to far off places

- Completing a degree

- Retirement

If you have other goals that you would like to achieve together with your husband, include them on your vision board as well. Write them well in advance so that whoever you meet will be able to help you realise them.

Priorities

Sometimes the life goals we set reflect our priorities, but this is not always the case. For instance, your goal could be to go for early retirement, but having children is an even bigger priority. In order to ensure that you and your husband are perfectly in sync, you should discuss the goals that are essential and the ones that are less urgent. The best way to communicate these priorities is to include them on the vision board.

FINAL THOUGHTS

The Love List

Congratulations on getting to this guide! You have unlocked the secret of how to choose your partner. I hope this guide has helped you to realise that everything you have imagined you wanted in a partner can be real in your life.

I hope you now realise how easy it is to visualise and put in perspective the things you need to consider when creating your partner. I am sure by now you feel confident and reinvigorated and that you can think more clearly about what it is you want and, more importantly, what you need in a partner.

By now you should know just how powerful you are and how powerful your mind can be. Remember it was Napoleon Hill that said, 'What the mind can conceive the mind can achieve.' This not only goes for choosing a partner in life but also for absolutely anything you put your mind to. Your destiny is in your hands and no one else's.

I encourage you to keep this book handy and revisit it whenever you need reminding of what to do and how to do it. Even when you just need a quick boost, it will always be here waiting for you.

When you have chosen the partner you so desire, pass this book on to a girlfriend who is still waiting to meet hers. Show her support, and tell her how helpful it was for you.

With all my Love,

Sonia

For a complete and free download of this Love List, head over to www.TheLoveListBook.com. Here you will find all the information you need to get hold of your perfect man, like right now. If you are older than 35, it doesn't mean that you cannot marry again. May be you were still pursuing your education or career, and that doesn't take away your right to get someone. There are good men out there. You only need to search correctly.

For Further Reading

When Love is Not Enough: 4 Tips for a Strong Relationship from Tiny Buddha

How to Find the Right Partner or Spouse WikiHow

How to Attract Amazing People Into Your Life by Michael Roderick

Other Resources

	Company	Website/Email
Website created by:	IODM	www.IODM.co.uk
Book Cover by:	IODM	www.IODM.co.uk
Book Edited by:	Ava Eagle Brown	www.AvaEagleBrown.com
Published by:	Ava Eagle Brown	www.AvaEagleBrown.com
Foreword by:	Claudine Reid MBE	www.ClaudineReid.co.uk
Ruby Antoine	A Calm Birth	www.ACalmBirth.com
Janet Blair	The Trading Floor	www.TheJanetBlair.com
Patrick Reid	PJ's Recruitment Services	www.PJsGroup.co.uk
Darren H Jones	Digital Marketer/Copy Writer	DarrenJones23@GoogleMail.com
Anthony King	PJ's Recruitment	www.PJsGroup.co.uk
Sharlette Reid	PJ's Recruitment	www.PJsGroup.co.uk
Lara Famosa	Gravity Angels	www.GravityAngels.com
Serah Lister	TV Recording Services	www.SerahLister.com
Matthew Lowe	Genesis Security Services	www.GenesisSecurity.co.uk/
Coach Lyken	Personal Trainer	www.Coach7CoreFitness.com

Wanna Be On Radio

Media Personality, Mentor, Award Winning Business and Communications Trainer, Published Author, Consultant, Inspirational Speaker and Voice Over Artist.

Sonia is the producer of Colourful Life morning show, which airs on the Award Winning Best Radio Station Colourful Radio every Tuesday and Wednesday.

With years of experience of working on radio, her journey into broadcasting has landed her in front of various high profiled guests.

Sonia interviews inspiring and successful people showcasing their strategies and principals for success.

She has interviewed President Barack Obama's former Social Secretary Desire Rogers, Levi Roots, Bianca Miller, Video Blogger Wally British to former Destiny's Child signer Michelle Williams.

Anyone looking to grow their business, enhance their skills, talents or expand their abilities should listen to her inspiring weekly shows. Sonia has a number ways to monetize your skills, one on one and group sessions available, (spaces are limited) so contact her today.

Interview me – if you want to get on radio, Sonia will teach you how to perform the best radio interview ever.

A-List Interviews –here she will teach you how to get high profile people to come on your show.

Become a Radio Host – Sonia will teach you how to create your own show and be a radio show host.